# Answers to Prayer

by

## Ellen G. White

**TEACH Services, Inc.**
*www.TEACHServices.com*

Copyright © 2008 TEACH Services, Inc.
ISBN-13:978-1-57258-523-2
Library of Congress Control Number: 2008928119

Published by
**TEACH Services, Inc.**
*www.TEACHServices.com*

*"One day alone is ours, and during this day we are to live for God. For this one day we are to place in the hand of Christ, in solemn service, all our purposes and plans, casting all our care upon Him, for He careth for us.*

*" 'I know the thoughts that I think toward you, saith the Lord, thoughts of peace, and not of evil, to give you an expected end.' 'In returning and rest shall ye be saved; in quietness and in confidence shall be your strength.' Jeremiah 29:11; Isaiah 30:15.*

*"If you will seek the Lord and be converted every day; if you will of your own spiritual choice be free and joyous in God; if with gladsome consent of heart to His gracious call you come wearing the yoke of Christ,—the yoke of obedience and service,—all your murmurings will be stilled, all your difficulties will be removed, all the perplexing problems that now confront you will be solved."*

—*Mount of Blessing, p. 101*

# Introduction

The question is often asked, "How can I pray so my prayers will be answered?" There are indeed answers, and in this book you will find a remarkable number of them.

In the pages before you, will be found an in-depth presentation of Spirit of Prophecy statements on this subject. Because it is a practical question, dealing with the everyday realities of life, the answers will also be found to be very practical, and will touch on a variety of points. Yet basic principles are also given, principles which underlie all genuine contact with God.

Our kind Father is more willing to give good gifts to His children than we are to receive them. On our part, there should be an earnestness to plead for help, a steadfast determination to cling to Him in spite of all that might occur, and a submission to His wise decisions.

We often ask for that which we do not need, and we generally want our prayers answered very soon. Yet our wonderful Father knows that prayer, continued over a period of time, prepares us to better receive the best gift, which may not actually be that which we are asking for. In many respects, the praying frequently helps us more than do the answers! Yet, in every instance in which we pray for deliverance from Satan's power and victory over sin, Christ sends His angels to more rapidly fulfill our request—but only to the degree to which our desire for that freedom is full and deep.

Never stop praying; it is your link with Heaven. In and of yourself, there will never be the strength or wisdom to do that which is needed. But, connected with Christ, you can do all that He asks of you.

In this study, we have not used the common method of quoting snatches here and there. Instead, when a passage of several paragraphs deals with the topic of how to obtain answers to prayer, the complete passage has been kept together.

In these deeply spiritual—yet very practical—statements, you will find an open door to the throne of God.

— *The Publishers*

**He will answer prayer**—"The Lord is acquainted with your situation. Nothing escapes His notice. He will hear your prayers; for He is a prayer-hearing and a prayer-answering God. Put your trust in Him, and He will certainly bring relief, in His own way."—*Evangelism,* p. 392:4.

**If you will find time**—"If you will find voice and time to pray, God will find time and voice to answer."—*My Life Today,* p. 16:5.

**The moment when help is nearest**—"To all who are reaching out to feel the guiding hand of God, the moment of greatest discouragement is the time when divine help is nearest . . From every temptation and every trial He will bring them forth with firmer faith and a richer experience."—*Sons and Daughters of God,* p. 92:5.

**Faith is trusting God**—"Faith is trusting God,—believing that He loves us, and knows best what is for our good. Thus, instead of our own, it leads us to choose His way. In place of our ignorance, it accepts His wisdom; in place of our weakness, His strength; in place of our sinfulness, His righteousness. Our lives, ourselves, are already His; faith acknowledges His ownership and accepts its blessing. Truth, uprightness, purity, have been pointed out as secrets of life's success. It is faith that puts us in possession of these principles.

"Every good impulse or aspiration is the gift of God; faith receives from God the life that alone can produce true growth and efficiency.

"How to exercise faith should be made very plain. To every promise of God there are conditions. If we are willing to do His will, all His strength is ours. Whatever gift He promises, is in the promise itself. 'The seed is the word of God.' Luke 8:11. As surely as the oak is in the acorn, so surely is the gift of God in His promise. If we receive the promise, we have the gift.

"Faith that enables us to receive God's gifts is itself a gift, of which some measure is imparted to every human being. It grows as exercised in appropriating the word of God. In order to strengthen faith, we must often bring it in contact with the word.

"In the study of the Bible the student should be led to see the power of God's word. In the creation, 'He spake, and it was done; He commanded, and it stood fast.' He 'calleth those things which be not as though they were' (Psalm 33:9; Romans 4:17); for when He calls them, they are.

"How often those who trusted the word of God, though in themselves utterly helpless, have withstood the power of the whole world—Enoch, pure in heart, holy in life, holding fast his faith in the triumph of righteousness against a corrupt and scoffing generation; Noah and his household against the men of his time, men of the greatest physical and mental strength and the most debased in morals; the children of Israel at the Red Sea, a helpless, terrified multitude of slaves, against the mightiest army of the mightiest nation on the globe; David, a shepherd lad, having God's promise of the throne, against Saul, the established monarch, bent on holding fast his power; Shadrach and his companions in the fire, and Nebuchadnezzar on the throne; Daniel among the lions, his enemies in the high places of the kingdom; Jesus on the cross, and the Jewish priests and rulers forcing even the Roman governor to work their will; Paul in chains  led to a criminal's death, Nero the despot of a world empire.

"Such examples are not found in the Bible only. They abound in every record of human progress. The Vaudois and the Huguenots, Wycliffe and Huss, Jerome and Luther, Tyndale and Knox, Zinzendorf and Wesley, with multitudes of others, have witnessed to the power of God's word against human power and policy in support of evil. These are the world's true nobility. This is its royal line. In this line the youth of today are called to take their places.

"Faith is needed in the smaller no less than in the greater affairs of life. In all our daily interests and occupations the sustaining strength of God becomes real to us through an abiding trust."—*Education,* pp. 253:1–255:1.

**Commit thy way to the Lord**—"Let the self-distrustful, whose lack of self-reliance leads them to shrink from care and responsibility, be taught reliance upon God. Thus many a one who otherwise would be but a cipher in the world, perhaps only a helpless burden, will be able to say with the apostle Paul, 'I can do all things through Christ which strengthens me . . . .

" 'Commit thy way unto the Lord; trust also in Him; and He shall bring it to pass . . . He shall bring forth thy righteousness as the light, and thy judgment as the noonday.' Psalm 37:5–6.

" 'The Lord also will be a refuge for the oppressed, a refuge in times of trouble. And they that know Thy name will put their trust in Thee: for Thou, Lord, hast not forsaken them that seek Thee.' Psalm 9:9–10.

"The compassion that God manifests toward us, He bids us manifest toward others. Let the impulsive, the self-sufficient, the revengeful, behold the meek and lowly One, led as a lamb to the slaughter, unretaliating as a sheep dumb before her shearers. Let them look upon Him whom our sins have pierced and our sorrows burdened, and they will learn to endure, to forbear, and to forgive.

"Through faith in Christ, every deficiency of character may be supplied, every defilement cleansed, every fault corrected, every excellence developed."—*Education*, pp. 256:2–257:2-5.

**Here is how it is done**—"Prayer and faith are closely allied, and they need to be studied together. In the prayer of faith there is a divine science; it is a science that every one who would make his lifework a success must understand. Christ says, 'What things soever ye desire, when ye pray, believe that ye receive them, and ye shall have them.' Mark 11:24. He makes it plain that our asking must be according to God's will; we must ask for the things that He has promised, and whatever we receive must be used in doing His will. The conditions met, the promise is unequivocal.

"For the pardon of sin, for the Holy Spirit, for a Christlike temper, for wisdom and strength to do His work, for any gift He has promised, we may ask; then we are to believe that we receive, and return thanks to God that we have received.

"We need look for no outward evidence of the blessing. The gift is in the promise, and we may go about our work assured that what God has promised He is able to perform, and that the gift, which we already possess, will be realized when we need it most.

"To live thus by the word of God means the surrender to Him of the whole life. There will be felt a continual sense of need and dependence, a drawing out of the heart after God. Prayer is a necessity; for it is the life of the soul. Family prayer, public prayer, have their place; but it is secret communion with God that sustains the soul life.

"It was in the mount with God that Moses beheld the pattern of that wonderful building which was to be the abiding place of His glory. It is in the mount with God—in the secret place of communion—that we are to contemplate His glorious ideal for humanity. Thus we shall be enabled so to fashion our character building that to us may be fulfilled His promise, 'I will dwell in them, and walk in them; and I will be their God, and they shall be My people.' 2 Cor 6:16.

"It was in hours of solitary prayer that Jesus in His earth life received wisdom and power. Let the youth follow His example in finding at dawn and twilight a quiet season for communion with their Father in heaven. And throughout the day let them lift up their hearts to God. At every step of our way He says, 'I the Lord thy God will hold thy right hand . . Fear not; I will help thee.' Isa 41:13. Could our children learn these lessons in the morning of their years, what freshness and power, what joy and sweetness, would be brought into their lives!"—*Education,* pp. 257:7–259:1.

**Answers from the Father through Jesus**—"The simple prayers indited by the Holy Spirit will ascend through the gates ajar, the open door which Christ has declared: I have opened, and no man can shut. These prayers, mingled with the incense of the perfection of Christ, will ascend as fragrance to the Father, and answers will come."—*6 Testimonies,* p. 467:4.

**The need for perseverance in prayer**—"I saw that there was a great lack of faith with the servants of God, as well as with the church. They were too easily discouraged, too ready to doubt God, too willing to believe that they had a hard lot and that God had forsaken them. I saw that this was cruel. God so loved them as to give His dearly beloved Son to die for them, and all heaven was interested in their salvation; yet after all that had been done for them, it was hard to believe and trust so kind and good a Father. He has said that He is more willing to give the Holy Spirit to them that ask Him, than earthly parents are to give good gifts to their children. I saw that the servants of God and the church were too easily discouraged. When they asked their Father in heaven for things which they thought they needed, and these did not immediately come, their faith wavered, their courage fled, and a murmuring feeling took possession of them. This, I saw, displeased God.

"Every saint who comes to God with a true heart, and sends his honest petitions to Him in faith, will have his prayers answered. Your faith must not let go of the promises of God, if you do not see or feel the immediate answer to your prayers. Be not afraid to trust God. Rely upon His sure promise: 'Ask, and ye shall receive.' God is too wise to err, and too good to withhold any good thing from His saints that walk uprightly. Man is erring, and although his petitions are sent up from an honest heart, he does not always ask for the things that are good for himself, or that will glorify God. When this is so, our wise and good

Father hears our prayers, and will answer, sometimes immediately; but He gives us the things that are for our best good and His own glory. God gives us blessings; if we could look into His plan, we would clearly see that He knows what is best for us and that our prayers are answered. Nothing hurtful is given, but the blessing we need, in the place of something we asked for that would not be good for us, but to our hurt.

"I saw that if we do not feel immediate answers to our prayers, we should hold fast our faith, not allowing distrust to come in, for that will separate us from God. If our faith wavers, we shall receive nothing from Him. Our confidence in God should be strong; and when we need it most, the blessing will fall upon us like a shower of rain.

"When the servants of God pray for His Spirit and blessing, it sometimes comes immediately; but it is not always then bestowed. At such times, faint not. Let your faith hold fast the promise that it will come. Let your trust be fully in God, and often that blessing will come when you need it most, and you will unexpectedly receive help from God when you are presenting the truth to unbelievers, and will be enabled to speak the word with clearness and power.

"It was represented to me like children asking a blessing of their earthly parents who love them. They ask something that the parent knows will hurt them; the parent gives them the things that will be good and healthful for them, in the place of that which they desired. I saw that every prayer which is sent up in faith from an honest heart will be heard of God and answered, and the one that sent up the petition will have the blessing when he needs it most, and it will often exceed his expectations. Not a prayer of a true saint is lost if sent up in faith from an honest heart."—*1 Testimonies,* pp. 120:1–121:3.

**Press into the presence of God—** "The people of God must move understandingly. They should not be satisfied until every known sin is confessed; then it is their privilege and duty to believe that Jesus accepts them. They must not wait for others to press through the darkness and obtain the victory for them to enjoy. Such enjoyment will last only till the meeting closes. But God must be served from principle instead of from feeling. Morning and night obtain the victory for yourselves in your own family. Let not your daily labor keep you from this. Take time to pray, and as you pray, believe that God hears you. Have faith mixed with your prayers. You may not at all times feel the immediate answer; but then it is that faith is tried. You are proved to see whether you will trust in God, whether you have living, abiding faith. 'Faithful is He that calleth you, who also will do it.' Walk the narrow plank of faith. Trust all on the promises of the Lord. Trust God in darkness. That is the time to have faith. But you often let feeling govern you. You look for worthiness in yourselves when you do not feel comforted by the Spirit of God, and despair because you cannot find it. You do not trust enough in Jesus, precious Jesus. You do not make His worthiness to be all, all. The very best you can do will not merit the favor of God. It is Jesus' worthiness that will save you, His blood that will cleanse you. But you have efforts to make. You must do what you can on your part. Be zealous and repent, then believe.

"Confound not faith and feeling together. They are distinct. Faith is ours to exercise. This faith we must keep in exercise. Believe, believe. Let your faith take hold of the blessing, and it is yours. Your feelings have nothing to do with this faith. When faith brings the blessing to your heart, and you rejoice in the blessing, it is no more faith, but feeling."—*1 Testimonies,* p. 167:1–2.

**Faith is needed, not presumption—** "God does not require His people to imitate Baal's prophets, to afflict their bodies and cry out and shout, and throw themselves into almost every attitude, having no regard for order, until their strength fails through sheer exhaustion. Religion does not consist in making a noise; yet when the soul is filled with the Spirit of the Lord, sweet, heartfelt praise to God glorifies Him. Some have professed to have great faith in God, and to have special gifts and special answers to their prayers, although the evidence was lacking. They mistook presumption for faith. The prayer of faith is never lost; but to claim that it will be always answered in the very way and for the particular thing we have expected, is presumption."—*1 Testimonies,* p. 231:1.

**Do not waver**—" 'If any of you lack wisdom, let him ask of God, that giveth to all men liberally, and upbraideth not; and it shall be given him.' Now the condition: 'But let him ask in faith, nothing wavering. For he that wavereth is like a wave of the sea driven with the wind and tossed. For let not that man think that he shall receive anything of the Lord.' This petition for wisdom is not to be a meaningless prayer, out of mind as soon as finished. It is a prayer that expresses the strong, earnest desire of the heart, arising from a conscious lack of wisdom to determine the will of God.

"After the prayer is made, if the answer is not realized immediately, do not weary of waiting and become unstable. Waver not. Cling to the promise, 'Faithful is He that calleth you, who also will do it.' Like the importunate widow, urge your case, being firm in your purpose. Is the object important and of great consequence to you? It certainly is. Then waver not, for your faith may be tried. If the thing you desire is valuable, it is worthy of a strong, earnest effort. You have the promise; watch and pray. Be steadfast and the prayer will be answered; for is it not God who has promised? If it costs you something to obtain it you will prize it the more when obtained. You are plainly told that if you waver you need not think that you shall receive anything of the Lord. A caution is here given not to become weary, but to rest firmly upon the promise. If you ask, He will give you liberally and upbraid not.

"Here is where many make a mistake. They waver from their purpose, and their faith fails. This is the reason they receive nothing of the Lord, who is our Source of strength. None need go in darkness, stumbling along like a blind man; for the Lord has provided light if they will accept it in His appointed way, and not choose their own way. He requires of all a diligent performance of everyday duties."—*2 Testimonies,* pp. 130:1–131:2.

**Iniquity must be cast out**—"With fasting and earnest prayer, with deep heart searching, stern self-examination, lay bare the soul; let no act escape your critical examination. Then, with self dead and your life hid with Christ in God, offer your humble petitions. If you regard iniquity in your heart, the Lord will not hear you. If He had heard your prayers, you would have been exalted. Satan has stood by, prepared to make the most of the advantage he has gained."—*2 Testimonies,* p. 158:0.

**Do all you can**—"Time is short, and you have no time to delay the preparation of heart necessary to labor earnestly and faithfully for your own soul, and for the salvation of your friends and neighbors, and all who come under your influence. Ever aim to so live in the light that your influence can be sanctifying upon those with whom you are associated in a business capacity or in common intercourse. There is fullness in Jesus. You can obtain strength from Him which will qualify you to walk even as He walked, but there must be no separation of affections from Him. He requires the entire man, the soul, body, and spirit. When you do all on your part which He requires, He will work for you, and bless and strengthen you by His rich grace."—*2 Testimonies,* pp. 155:3–156:0.

**Watch, pray, and work**—"There is strength to be obtained of God. He can help.

He can give grace and heavenly wisdom. If you ask in faith, you will receive; but you must watch unto prayer. Watch, pray, and work, should be your watchword."—*2 Testimonies*, p. 427:0.

**Not always according to your expectations**—"He permitted you to pass through real trials and feel privation and want, that you might know how to exercise pity and sympathy, and tender love for the unfortunate and oppressed, and for those borne down with want and passing through trial and affliction.

"While you prayed in your affliction for peace in Christ, a cloud of darkness seemed to blacken across your mind. The rest and peace did not come as you expected. At times your faith seemed to be tested to the utmost. As you looked back to your past life, you saw sorrow and disappointment; as you viewed the future, all was uncertainty. The divine Hand led you wondrously to bring you to the cross and to teach you that God was indeed a rewarder of those who diligently seek Him. Those who ask aright will receive. He that seeketh in faith shall find. The experience gained in the furnace of trial and affliction is worth more than all the inconvenience and painful experience it costs.

"The prayers that you offered in your loneliness, in your weariness and trial, God answered, not always according to your expectations, but for your good."—*3 Testimonies,* p. 415:1–3.

**Never let your courage fail**—"God's workers will meet with turmoil, discomfort, and weariness. At times, uncertain and distracted, they are almost in despair. When this restless nervousness comes, let them remember Christ's invitation: 'Come ye yourselves apart, . . . and rest awhile.' The Saviour 'giveth power to the faint; and to them that have no might He increaseth strength.' Isa. 40:29.

"Difficulties will arise that will try your faith and patience. Face them bravely. Look on the bright side. If the work is hindered, be sure that it is not your fault, and then go forward, rejoicing in the Lord. Heaven is full of joy. It resounds with the praises of Him who made so wonderful a sacrifice for the redemption of the human race. Should not the church on earth be full of praise? Should not Christians publish throughout the world the joy of serving Christ? Those who in heaven join with the angelic choir in their anthem of praise must learn on earth the song of heaven, the keynote of which is thanksgiving.

"Never let your courage fail. Never talk unbelief because appearances are against you. As you work for the Master you will feel pressure for want of means, but the Lord will hear and answer your petitions for help. Let your language be: 'The Lord God will help me; therefore shall I not be confounded: therefore have I set my face like a flint, and I know that I shall not be ashamed.' Isa. 50:7.

"If you make a mistake, turn your defeat into victory. The lessons that God sends will always, if well learned, bring help in due time. Put your trust in God. Pray much, and believe. Trusting, hoping, believing, holding fast the hand of Infinite Power, you will be more than conquerors.

"True workers walk and work by faith. Sometimes they grow weary with watching the slow advance of the work when the battle wages strong between the powers of good and evil. But if they refuse to fail or be discouraged they will see the clouds breaking away and the promise of deliverance fulfilling. Through the mist with which Satan has surrounded them, they will see the shining of the bright beams of the Sun of Righteousness.

"Work in faith, and leave results with God. Pray in faith, and the mystery of His providence will bring its answer. At times it may seem that you cannot succeed. But work and believe, putting into your efforts faith, hope, and courage. After doing what you can, wait for the Lord, declaring His faithfulness, and He will bring His word to pass. Wait, not in fretful anxiety, but in undaunted faith and unshaken trust.

" 'If God be for us, who can be against us? He that spared not His own Son, but delivered Him up for us all, how shall He not with Him also freely give us all things? . . . Who shall separate us from the love of Christ? shall tribulation, or distress, or persecution, or famine, or nakedness, or peril, or sword? . . . Nay, in all these things we are more than conquerors through Him that loved us. For I am persuaded, that neither death, nor life, nor angels, nor principalities, nor powers, nor things present, nor things to come, nor height, nor depth, nor any other creature, shall be able to separate us from the love of God, which is in Christ Jesus our Lord.' "—7 *Testimonies,* pp. 244:1–245:3.

**He persevered until the answer came**—"Important lessons are presented to us in the experience of Elijah. When upon Mt. Carmel he offered the prayer for rain, his faith was tested, but he persevered in making known his request unto God. Six times he prayed earnestly, and yet there was no sign that his petition was granted, but with a strong faith he urged his plea to the throne of grace. Had he given up in discouragement at the sixth time, his prayer would not have been answered, but he persevered till the answer came. We have a God whose ear is not closed to our petitions; and if we prove His word, He will honor our faith. He wants us to have all our interests interwoven with His interests, and then He can safely bless us; for we shall not then take glory to self when the blessing is ours, but shall render all the praise to God. God does not always answer our prayers the first time we call upon Him; for should He do this, we might take it for granted that we had a right to all the blessings and favors He bestowed upon us. Instead of searching our hearts to see if any evil was entertained by us, any sin indulged, we should become careless, and fail to realize our dependence upon Him, and our need of His help.

"Elijah humbled himself until he was in a condition where he would not take the glory to himself. This is the condition upon which the Lord hears prayer, for then we shall give the praise to Him. The custom of offering praise to men is one that results in great evil. One praises another, and thus men are led to feel that glory and honor belong to them. When you exalt man, you lay a snare for his soul, and do just as Satan would have you. You should praise God with all your heart, soul, might, mind, and strength; for God alone is worthy to be glorified. (Review and Herald, March 27, 1913)."—*2 Bible Commentary,* pp. 1034/2:3–1035:1.

**Those who do not realize the intensity of the work**—"Satan seeks continually to block the way, so that the truth shall be bound about by human devising; and those who have light and knowledge are in the greatest danger unless they constantly consecrate themselves to God, humiliating self, and realizing the peril of the times.

"Heavenly beings are appointed to answer the prayers of those who are working unselfishly for the interests of the cause of God. The very highest angels in the heavenly courts are appointed to work out the prayers which ascend to God for the advancement of the cause of God. Each angel has his particular post of duty, which he is not permitted to leave for any other place. If he should leave, the powers of darkness would gain an advantage . . . .

"Day by day the conflict between good and evil is going on. Why is it that those who have had many opportunities and advantages do not realize the intensity of this work? They should be intelligent in regard to this. God is the Ruler. By His supreme power He holds in check and controls earthly potentates. Through His agencies He does the work which was ordained before the foundation of the world.

"As a people we do not understand as we should the great conflict going on between invisible agencies, the controversy between loyal and disloyal angels. Evil angels are constantly at work, planning their line of attack, controlling as commanders, kings, and rulers, the disloyal human forces . . . I call upon the ministers of Christ to press home upon the understanding of all who come within the reach of their voice, the truth of the ministration of angels. Do not indulge in fanciful speculations. The written Word is our only safety. We must pray as did Daniel, that we may be guarded by heavenly intelligences. As ministering spirits angels are sent forth to minister to those who shall be heirs of salvation. Pray, my brethren, pray as you have never prayed before. We are not prepared for the Lord's coming. We need to make thorough work for eternity (Letter 201, 1899)."—*4 Bible Commentary,* p. 1173/2:0–3.

**Be intensely in earnest to do God's will**—"In the Word of God are represented two contending parties that influence and control human agencies in our world. Constantly these parties are working with every human being. Those who are under God's control and who are influenced by the heavenly angels, will be able to discern the crafty workings of the unseen powers of darkness. Those who desire to be in harmony with the heavenly agencies should be intensely in earnest to do God's will. They must give no place whatever to Satan and his angels.

"But unless we are constantly on guard, we shall be overcome by the enemy. Although a solemn revelation of God's will concerning us has been revealed to all, yet a knowledge of His will does not set aside the necessity of offering earnest supplications to Him for help, and of diligently seeking to cooperate with Him in answering the prayers offered. He accomplishes His purposes through human instrumentalities (MS 95, 1903)."—*6 Bible Commentary,* p. 1119/1:1–2.

**Plead His promises**—"Satan had accused Jacob before the angels of God, claiming the right to destroy him because of his sin; he had moved upon Esau to march against him; and during the patriarch's long night of wrestling, Satan endeavored to force upon him a sense of his guilt, in order to discourage him, and break his hold upon God. When in his distress Jacob laid hold of the Angel, and made supplication with tears, the heavenly Messenger, in order to try his faith, also reminded him of his sin, and endeavored to escape from him. But Jacob would not be turned away. He had learned that God is merciful, and he cast himself upon His mercy. He pointed back to his repentance for his sin, and pleaded for deliverance. As he reviewed his life, he was driven almost to despair; but he held fast the Angel, and with earnest, agonizing cries urged his petition until he prevailed.

"Such will be the experience of God's people in their final struggle with the powers of evil. God will test their faith, their perseverance, their confidence in His power to deliver them. Satan will endeavor to terrify them with the thought that their cases are hopeless; that their sins have been too great to receive pardon. They will have a deep sense of their shortcomings, and as they review their lives their hopes will sink. But remembering the greatness of God's mercy, and their own sincere repentance, they will plead His promises made through Christ to helpless, repenting sinners. Their faith will not fail because their prayers are not immediately answered. They will lay hold of the strength of God, as Jacob laid hold of the Angel, and the language of their souls will be, 'I will not let Thee go, except Thou bless me.'

"Had not Jacob previously repented of his sin in obtaining the birthright by fraud, God could not have heard his prayer and mercifully preserved his life. So in the time of trouble, if the people of God had unconfessed sins to appear before them while tortured with fear and anguish, they would be overwhelmed; despair would cut off their faith, and they could not have confidence to plead with God for deliverance. But while they have a deep sense of their unworthiness, they will have no concealed wrongs to reveal. Their sins will have been blotted out by the atoning blood of Christ, and they cannot bring them to remembrance.

"Satan leads many to believe that God will overlook their unfaithfulness in the minor affairs of life; but the Lord shows in His dealing with Jacob that He can in no wise sanction or tolerate evil. All who endeavor to excuse or conceal their sins, and permit them to remain upon the books of heaven, unconfessed and unforgiven, will be overcome by Satan. The more exalted their profession, and the more honorable the position which they hold, the more grievous is their course in the sight of God, and the more certain the triumph of the great adversary.

"Yet Jacob's history is an assurance that God will not cast off those who have been betrayed into sin, but who have returned unto Him with true repentance. It was by self-surrender and confiding faith that Jacob gained what he had failed to gain by conflict in his own strength. God thus taught His servant that divine power and grace alone could give him the blessing he craved. Thus it will be with those who live in the last days. As dangers surround them, and despair seizes upon the soul, they must depend solely upon the merits of the atonement. We can do nothing of ourselves. In all our helpless unworthiness we must trust in the merits of the crucified and risen Saviour. None will ever perish while they do this. The long, black catalogue of our delinquencies is before the eye of the Infinite. The register is complete; none of our offenses are forgotten. But He who listened to the cries of His servants of old, will hear the prayer of faith and pardon our transgressions. He has promised, and He will fulfill His word.

"Jacob prevailed because he was persevering and determined. His experience testifies to the power of importunate prayer. It is now that we are to learn this lesson of prevailing prayer, of unyielding faith. The greatest victories to the church of Christ or to the individual Christian are not those that are gained by talent or education, by wealth or the favor of men. They are those victories that are gained in the audience chamber with God, when earnest, agonizing faith lays hold upon the mighty arm of power." —*Patriarchs and Prophets,* pp. 201:3–203:1.

**Why He delays the answer**—"He who blessed the nobleman at Capernaum is just as desirous of blessing us. But like the afflicted father, we are often led to seek Jesus by the desire for some earthly good; and upon the granting of our request we rest our confidence in His love. The Saviour longs to give us a greater blessing than we ask; and He delays the answer to our request that He may show us the evil of our own hearts, and our deep need of His grace. He desires us to renounce the selfishness that leads us to seek Him. Confessing our helplessness and bitter need, we are to trust ourselves wholly to His love.

"The nobleman wanted to see the fulfillment of his prayer before he should believe; but he had to accept the word of Jesus that his request was heard and the blessing granted. This lesson we also have to learn. Not because we see or feel that God hears us are we to believe. We are to trust in His promises. When we come to Him in faith, every petition enters the heart of God. When we have asked for His blessing, we should believe that we receive it, and thank Him that we have received it. Then we are to go about our duties, assured that the blessing will be realized when we need it most. When we have learned to do this, we shall know that our prayers are answered. God will do for us 'exceeding abundantly,' 'according to the riches of His glory,' and 'the working of His mighty power.' Eph. 3:20, 16; 1:19."—*Desire of Ages*, p. 200:3–4.

**No delay when we really want deliverance from sin**—"In some instances of healing, Jesus did not at once grant the blessing sought. But in the case of leprosy, no sooner was the appeal made than it was granted. When we pray for earthly blessings, the answer to our prayer may be delayed, or God may give us something other than we ask, but not so when we ask for deliverance from sin. It is His will to cleanse us from sin, to make us His children, and to enable us to live a holy life. Christ 'gave Himself for our sins, that He might deliver us from this present evil world, according to the will of God and our Father.' And 'this is the confidence that we have in Him, that, if we ask anything according to His will, He heareth us; and if we know that He hear us, whatsoever we ask, we know that we have the petitions that we desire of Him.' 1 John 5:14, 15. 'If we confess our sins, He is faithful and just to forgive us our sins, and to cleanse us from all unrighteousness.' 1 John 1:9."—*Desire of Ages,* p. 266:2.

**He answers the prayers of the meek**—" 'This is the confidence that we have in Him, that, if we ask anything according to His will, He heareth us: and if we know that He hear us, whatsoever we ask, we know that we have the petitions that we desired of Him.' God has appointed the angels that do His will to respond to the prayers of the meek of the earth, and to guide His ministers with counsel and judgment. Heavenly agencies are constantly seeking to impart grace and strength and counsel to God's faithful children, that they may act their part in the work of communicating light to the world. The wonderful sacrifice of Christ has made it possible for every man to do a special work. When the worker receives wisdom from the only true source, he will become a pure channel of light and blessing; for he will receive his capability for service in rich currents of grace and light from the throne of God."—*Testimonies to Ministers,* p. 484:2.

**Let us pray for the sick**—"Let us study our Bibles, and teach the words of truth. Let us do as Christ's apostles did; let us offer prayer for the sick, for there are many who cannot have the advantages of our sanitariums. The Lord will remove infirmities in answer to prayer. Gospel ministers should be able to present the subject of health reform in its simplicity. If this phase of present truth is presented in a clear, simple, Christlike manner, it will have an effect upon the people. There will be a response from many hearts.—Letter 128, 1909."—*Medical Ministry*, p. 242:2.

**Not just prayer, but also natural remedies**—"Some have asked me, 'Why should we have sanitariums? Why should we not, like Christ, pray for the sick, that they may be healed miraculously?' I have answered, 'Suppose we were able to do this in all cases; how many would appreciate the healing? Would those who were healed become health reformers, or continue to be health destroyers?'

"Jesus Christ is the Great Healer, but He desires that by living in conformity with His laws we may cooperate with Him in the recovery and the maintenance of health. Combined with the work of healing there must be an imparting of knowledge of how to resist temptations. Those who come to our sanitariums should be aroused to a sense of their own responsibility to work in harmony with the God of truth.

"We cannot heal. We cannot change the diseased conditions of the body. But it is our part, as medical missionaries, as workers together with God, to use the means that He has provided. Then we should pray that God will bless these agencies. We do believe in a God; we believe in a God who hears and answers prayer. He has said, 'Ask, and ye shall receive; seek, and ye shall find; knock, and it shall be opened unto you.' "—*Medical Ministry,* p. 13:1–3.

**We must also do our part**—"Many have expected that God would keep them from sickness merely because they have asked Him to do so. But God did not regard their prayers, because their faith was not made perfect by works. God will not work a miracle to keep those from sickness who have no care for themselves, but are continually violating the laws of health and make no efforts to prevent disease. When we do all we can on our part to have health, then may we expect that the blessed results will follow, and we can ask God in faith to bless our efforts for the preservation of health. He will then answer our prayer, if His name can be glorified thereby. But let all understand that they have a work to do. God will not work in a miraculous manner to preserve the health of persons who are taking a sure course to make themselves sick, by their careless inattention to the laws of health.

"Those who will gratify their appetite, and then suffer because of their intemperance, and take drugs to relieve them, may be assured that God will not interpose to save health and life which are so recklessly periled. The cause has produced the effect. Many, as their last resort, follow the directions in the word of God, and request the prayers of the elders of the church for their restoration to health. God does not see fit to answer prayers offered in behalf of such, for He knows that if they should be restored to health, they would again sacrifice it upon the altar of unhealthy appetite."—*Medical Ministry,* pp. 13:4–14:1.

**Wrongdoing must be stopped**—"It is labor lost to teach people to look to God as a healer of their infirmities, unless they are taught also to lay aside unhealthful practices. In order to receive His blessing in answer to prayer, they must cease to do evil and learn to do well. Their surroundings must be sanitary, their habits of life correct. They must live in harmony with the law of God, both natural and spiritual.

"To those who desire prayer for their restoration to health, it should be made plain that the violation of God's law, either natural or spiritual, is sin, and that in order for them to receive His blessing, sin must be confessed and forsaken.

"The Scripture bids us, 'Confess your faults one to another, and pray one for another, that ye may be healed.' James 5:16. To the one asking for prayer, let thoughts like these be presented: 'We cannot read the heart, or know the secrets of your life. These are known only to yourself and to God. If you repent of your sins, it is your duty to make confession of them.' Sin of a private character is to be confessed to Christ, the only mediator between God and man. For 'if any man sin, we have an advocate with the Father, Jesus Christ the righteous.' 1 John 2:1. Every sin is an offense against God and is to be confessed to Him through Christ. Every open sin should be as openly confessed. Wrong done to a fellow being should be made right with the one who has been offended. If any who are seeking health have been guilty of evilspeaking, if they have sowed discord in the home, the neighborhood, or the church, and have stirred up alienation and dissension, if by any wrong practice they have led others into sin, these things should be confessed before God and before those who have been offended. 'If we confess our sins, He is faithful and just to forgive us our sins, and to cleanse us from all unrighteousness.' 1 John 1:9.

"When wrongs have been righted, we may present the needs of the sick to the Lord in calm faith, as His Spirit may indicate. He knows each individual by name, and cares for each as if there were not another upon the earth for whom He gave His beloved Son. Because God's love is so great and so unfailing, the sick should be encouraged to trust in Him and be cheerful. To be anxious about themselves tends to cause weakness and disease. If they will rise above depression and gloom, their prospect of recovery will be better; for 'the eye of the Lord is upon them' 'that hope in His mercy.' Psalm 33:18.

"In prayer for the sick it should be remembered that 'we know not what we should pray for as we ought.' Romans 8:26. We do not know whether the blessing we desire will be best or not. Therefore our prayers should include this thought: 'Lord, thou knowest every secret of the soul. Thou art acquainted with these persons. Jesus, their Advocate, gave His life for them. His love for them is greater than ours can possibly be. If, therefore, it is for Thy glory and the good of the afflicted ones, we ask, in the name of Jesus, that they may be restored to health. If it be not Thy will that they may be restored, we ask that Thy grace may comfort and Thy presence sustain them in their sufferings.'

"God knows the end from the beginning. He is acquainted with the hearts of all men. He reads every secret of the soul. He knows whether those for whom prayer is offered would or would not be able to endure the trials that would come upon them should they live. He knows whether their lives would be a blessing or a curse to themselves and to the world. This is one reason why, while presenting our petitions with earnestness, we should say, 'Nevertheless not my will, but Thine, be done.' Luke 22:42. Jesus added these words of submission to the wisdom and will of God when in the Garden of Gethsemane He pleaded,

'O My Father, if it be possible, let this cup pass from Me.' Matthew 26:39. And if they were appropriate for Him, the Son of God, how much more are they becoming on the lips of finite, erring mortals!

"The consistent course is to commit our desires to our all-wise heavenly Father, and then, in perfect confidence, trust all to Him. We know that God hears us if we ask according to His will. But to press our petitions without a submissive spirit is not right; our prayers must take the form, not of command, but of intercession.

"There are cases where God works decidedly by His divine power in the restoration of health. But not all the sick are healed. Many are laid away to sleep in Jesus. John on the Isle of Patmos was bidden to write: 'Blessed are the dead which die in the Lord from henceforth: Yea, saith the Spirit, that they may rest from their labors; and their works do follow them.' Revelation 14:13. From this we see that if persons are not raised to health, they should not on this account be judged as wanting in faith.

"We all desire immediate and direct answers to our prayers, and are tempted to become discouraged when the answer is delayed or comes in an unlooked-for form. But God is too wise and good to answer our prayers always at just the time and in just the manner we desire. He will do more and better for us than to accomplish all our wishes. And because we can trust His wisdom and love, we should not ask Him to concede to our will, but should seek to enter into and accomplish His purpose. Our desires and interests should be lost in His will. These experiences that test faith are for our benefit. By them it is made manifest whether our faith is true and sincere, resting on the word of God alone, or whether depending on circumstances, it is uncertain and changeable. Faith is strengthened by exercise. We must let patience have its perfect work, remembering that there are precious promises in the Scriptures for those who wait upon the Lord.

"Not all understand these principles. Many who seek the Lord's healing mercy think that they must have a direct and immediate answer to their prayers or their faith is defective. For this reason, those who are weakened by disease need to be counseled wisely, that they may act with discretion. They should not disregard their duty to the friends who may survive them, or neglect to employ nature's agencies for the restoration of health.

"Often there is danger of error here. Believing that they will be healed in answer to prayer, some fear to do anything that might seem to indicate a lack of faith. But they should not neglect to set their affairs in order as they would desire to do if they expected to be removed by death. Nor should they fear to utter words of encouragement or counsel which at the parting hour they wish to speak to their loved ones.

"Those who seek healing by prayer should not neglect to make use of the remedial agencies within their reach. It is not a denial of faith to use such remedies as God has provided to alleviate pain and to aid nature in her work of restoration. It is no denial of faith to co-operate with God, and to place themselves in the condition most favorable to recovery. God has put it in our power to obtain a knowledge of the laws of life. This knowledge has been placed within our reach for use. We should employ every facility for the restoration of health, taking every advantage possible, working in harmony with natural laws. When we have prayed for the recovery of the sick, we can work with all the more energy, thanking God that we have the privilege of co-operating with Him, and asking His blessing on the means which He Himself has provided.

"We have the sanction of the word of God for the use of remedial agencies. Hezekiah, king of Israel, was sick, and a prophet of God brought him the message that he should die. He cried unto the Lord, and the Lord heard His servant and sent him a message that fifteen years should be added to his life. Now, one word from God would have healed Hezekiah instantly; but special directions were given, 'Let them take a lump of figs, and lay it for a plaster upon the boil, and he shall recover.' Isaiah 38:21.

"On one occasion Christ anointed the eyes of a blind man with clay and bade him, 'Go, wash in the pool of Siloam . . He went his way therefore, and washed, and came seeing.' John 9:7. The cure could be wrought only by the power of the Great Healer, yet Christ made use of the simple agencies of nature. While He did not give countenance to drug medication, He sanctioned the use of simple and natural remedies."—*Ministry of Healing,* pp. 227:4–233:1.

**Do not ask for unconditional healing**—"But it is not always safe to ask for unconditional healing. Let your prayer include this thought: 'Lord, Thou knowest every secret of the soul. Thou art acquainted with these persons; for Jesus, their advocate gave His life for them. He loves them better than we possibly can. If, therefore, it is for Thy glory and the good of these afflicted ones to raise them up to health, we ask Thee in the name of Jesus, that health may be given them at this time. In a petition of this kind, no lack of faith is manifested.' "—*Counsels on Health,* p. 375:1.

**How we are to pray for the sick**— "In the case of Sister F, there needed to be a great work accomplished. Those who united in praying for her needed a work done for them. Had God answered their prayers, it would have proved their ruin. In such cases of affliction, where Satan has control of the mind, before engaging in prayer there should be the closest self-examination to discover if there are not sins which need to be repented of, confessed, and forsaken. Deep humility of soul before God is necessary, and firm, humble reliance upon the merits of the blood of Christ alone. Fasting and prayer will accomplish nothing while the heart is estranged from God by a wrong course of action. 'Is not this the fast that I have chosen? to loose the bands of wickedness, to undo the heavy burdens, and to let the oppressed go free, and that ye break every yoke? Is it not to deal thy bread to the hungry, and that thou bring the poor that are cast out to thy house? when thou seest the naked, that thou cover him; and that thou hide not thyself from thine own flesh?' 'Then shalt thou call, and the Lord shall answer; thou shalt cry, and He shall say, Here I am. If thou take away from the midst of thee the yoke, the putting forth of the finger, and speaking vanity; and if thou draw out thy soul to the hungry, and satisfy the afflicted soul; then shall thy light rise in obscurity, and thy darkness be as the noonday: and the Lord shall guide thee continually, and satisfy thy soul in drought, and make fat thy bones: and thou shalt be like a watered garden, and like a spring of water, whose waters fail not.'

"It is heartwork that the Lord requires, good works springing from a heart filled with love. All should carefully and prayerfully consider the above scriptures, and investigate their motives and actions. The promise of God to us is on condition of obedience, compliance with all His requirements. 'Cry aloud,' saith the prophet Isaiah, 'spare not, lift up thy voice like a trumpet, and show My people their transgression, and the house of Jacob their sins. Yet they seek Me daily, and delight to know My ways, as a nation that did righteousness, and forsook not the ordinance of their God: they ask of Me the ordinances of justice; they take delight in approaching to God. Wherefore have we fasted, say they, and Thou seest not? wherefore have we afflicted our soul, and Thou takest no knowledge?'

"A people are here addressed who make high profession, who are in the habit of praying, and who delight in religious exercises; yet there is a lack. They realize that their prayers are not answered; their zealous, earnest efforts are not observed in heaven, and they earnestly inquire why the Lord makes them no returns. It is not because there is any neglect on the part of God. The difficulty is with the people. While professing godliness, they do not bear fruit to the glory of God; their works are not what they should be. They are living in neglect of positive duties. Unless these are performed, God cannot answer their prayers according to His glory. In the case of offering prayer for Sister F, there was confusion of sentiment. Some were fanatical and moved from impulse. They possessed a zeal, but not according to knowledge. Some looked at the great thing to be accomplished in this case and began to triumph before the victory was gained. There was much of the Jehu spirit manifested: 'Come with me, and see my zeal for the Lord.' In place of this self-confident assurance, the case should have been presented to God with a spirit of humbleness and distrustfulness of self, and with a broken and a contrite heart.

"I was shown that in case of sickness, where the way is clear for the offering up of prayer for the sick, the case should be committed to the Lord in calm faith, not with a storm of excitement. He alone is acquainted with the past life of the individual and knows what his future will be. He who is acquainted with the hearts of all men knows whether the person, if raised up, would glorify His name or dishonor Him by backsliding and apostasy. All that we are required to do is to ask God to raise the sick up if in accordance with His will, believing that He hears the reasons which we present and the fervent prayers offered. If the Lord sees it will best honor Him, He will answer our prayers. But to urge recovery without submission to His will is not right.

"What God promises He is able at any time to perform, and the work which He gives His people to do He is able to accomplish by them. If they will live according to every word He has spoken, every good word and promise will be fulfilled unto them. But if they come short of perfect obedience, the great and precious promises are afar off, and they cannot reach the fulfillment.

"All that can be done in praying for the sick is to earnestly importune God in their behalf, and in perfect confidence rest the matter in His hands. If we regard iniquity in our hearts the Lord will not hear us. He can do what He will with His own. He will glorify Himself by working in and through them who wholly follow Him, so that it shall be known that it is the Lord and that their works are wrought in God. Said Christ: 'If any man serve Me, him will My Father honor.' When we come to Him we should pray that we may enter into and accomplish His purpose, and that our desires and interests may be lost in His. We should acknowledge our acceptance of His will, not praying Him to concede to ours. It is better for us that God does not always answer our prayers just when we desire, and in just the manner we wish. He will do more and better for us than to accomplish all our wishes, for our wisdom is folly.

"We have united in earnest prayer around the sickbed of men, women, and children, and have felt that they were given back to us from the dead in answer to our earnest prayers. In these prayers we thought we must be positive and, if we exercised faith, that we must ask for nothing less than life. We dared not say, 'If it will glorify God,' fearing it would admit a semblance of doubt. We have anxiously watched those who have been given back, as it were, from the dead. We have seen some of these, especially youth, raised to health, and they have forgotten God, become dissolute in life, causing sorrow and anguish to parents and friends, and have become a shame to those who feared to pray. They lived not to honor and glorify God, but to curse Him with their lives of vice.

"We no longer mark out a way nor seek to bring the Lord to our wishes. If the life of the sick can glorify Him, we pray that they may live; nevertheless, not as we will but as He will. Our faith can be just as firm, and more reliable, by committing the desire to the all-wise God, and, without feverish anxiety, in perfect confidence, trusting all to Him. We have the promise. We know that He hears us if we ask according to His will. Our petitions must not take the form of a command, but of intercession for Him to do the things we desire of Him. When the church are united, they will have strength and power; but when part of them are united to the world, and many are given to covetousness, which God abhors, He can do but little for them. Unbelief and sin shut them away from God. We are so weak that we cannot bear much spiritual prosperity, lest we take the glory, and accredit goodness and righteousness to ourselves as the reason of the signal blessing of God, when it was all because of the great mercy and lovingkindness of our compassionate heavenly Father, and not because any good was found in us."—*2 Testimonies,* pp. 145:1–149:1.

**The sick also should seek to be a blessing to others**—"One of the surest hindrances to the recovery of the sick is the centering of attention upon themselves. Many invalids feel that everyone should give them sympathy and help, when what they need is to have their attention turned away from themselves, to think of and care for others.

"Often prayer is solicited for the afflicted, the sorrowful, the discouraged; and this is right. We should pray that God will shed light into the darkened mind and comfort the sorrowful heart. But God answers prayer for those who place themselves in the channel of His blessings. While we offer prayer for these sorrowful ones, we should encourage them to try to help those more needy than themselves. The darkness will be dispelled from their own hearts as they try to help others. As we seek to comfort others with the comfort wherewith we are comforted, the blessing comes back to us.

"The fifty-eighth chapter of Isaiah is a prescription for maladies of the body and of the soul. If we desire health and the true joy of life we must put into practice the rules given in this scripture."—*Ministry of Healing,* p. 256:1–3.

**After we have prayed for the sick—** "When we have prayed for the recovery of the sick, whatever the outcome of the case, let us not lose faith in God. If we are called upon to meet bereavement, let us accept the bitter cup, remembering that a Father's hand holds it to our lips. But should health be restored, it should not be forgotten that the recipient of healing mercy is placed under renewed obligation to the Creator."—*Ministry of Healing,* p. 233:2.

**When God says No**—"Our plans are not always God's plans. He may see that it is best for us and for His cause to refuse our very best intentions, as He did in the case of David. But of one thing we may be assured, He will bless and use in the advancement of His cause those who sincerely devote themselves and all they have to His glory. If He sees it best not to grant their desires He will counterbalance the refusal by giving them tokens of His love and entrusting to them another service.

"In His loving care and interest for us, often He who understands us better than we understand ourselves refuses to permit us selfishly to seek the gratification of our own ambition. He does not permit us to pass by the homely but sacred duties that lie next us. Often these duties afford the very training essential to prepare us for a higher work. Often our plans fail that God's plans for us may succeed.

"We are never called upon to make a real sacrifice for God. Many things He asks us to yield to Him, but in doing this we are but giving up that which hinders us in the heavenward way. Even when called upon to surrender those things which in themselves are good, we may be sure that

God is thus working out for us some higher good.

"In the future life the mysteries that here have annoyed and disappointed us will be made plain. We shall see that our seemingly unanswered prayers and disappointed hopes have been among our greatest blessings."—*Ministry of Healing,* pp. 473:2–474:1.

**Yielding to the decision to the Lord**—"When I pray earnestly for restoration, and it seems that the Lord does not answer, my spirit almost faints within me. Then it is that the dear Saviour makes me mindful of His presence. He says to me, Cannot you trust Him who has purchased you with His own blood? I have graven thee on the palms of My hands. Then my soul is nourished with the divine Presence. I am lifted out of myself, as it were, into the presence of God."—*2 Selected Messages,* p. 240:1.

**Conditions to answered prayer**—"God regards us as His children. He has redeemed us out of the careless world and has chosen us to become members of the royal family, sons and daughters of the heavenly King. He invites us to trust in

Him with a trust deeper and stronger than that of a child in his earthly father. Parents love their children, but the love of God is larger, broader, deeper, than human love can possibly be. It is immeasurable. Then if earthly parents know how to give good gifts to their children, how much more shall our Father in heaven give the Holy Spirit to those who ask Him?

"Christ's lessons in regard to prayer should be carefully considered. There is a divine science in prayer, and His illustration brings to view principles that all need to understand. He shows what is the true spirit of prayer, He teaches the necessity of perseverance in presenting our requests to God, and assures us of His willingness to hear and answer prayer.

"Our prayers are not to be a selfish asking, merely for our own benefit. We are to ask that we may give. The principle of Christ's life must be the principle of our lives. 'For their sakes,' He said, speaking of His disciples, 'I sanctify Myself, that they also might be sanctified.' John 17:19. The same devotion, the same self-sacrifice, the same subjection to the claims of the word of God, that were manifest in Christ, must be seen in His servants. Our mission to the world is not to serve or please ourselves; we are to glorify God by co-operating with Him to save sinners. We are to ask blessings from God that we may communicate to others. The capacity for receiving is preserved only by imparting. We cannot continue to receive heavenly treasure without communicating to those around us.

"In the parable the petitioner was again and again repulsed, but he did not relinquish his purpose. So our prayers do not always seem to receive an immediate answer; but Christ teaches that we should not cease to pray. Prayer is not to work any change in God; it is to bring us into harmony with God. When we make request of Him, He may see that it is necessary for us to search our hearts and repent of sin. Therefore He takes us through test and trial, He brings us through humiliation, that we may see what hinders the working of His Holy Spirit through us.

"There are conditions to the fulfillment of God's promises, and prayer can never take the place of duty. 'If ye love Me,' Christ says, 'Keep My commandments.' 'He that hath My commandments, and keepeth them, he it is that loveth Me; and he that loveth Me shall be loved of My Father, and I will love him, and will manifest Myself to him.' John 14:15, 21. Those who bring their petitions to God, claiming His promise while they do not comply with the conditions, insult Jehovah. They bring the name of Christ as their authority for the fulfillment of the promise, but they do not those things that would show faith in Christ and love for Him.

"Many are forfeiting the condition of acceptance with the Father. We need to examine closely the deed of trust wherewith we approach God. If we are disobedient, we bring to the Lord a note to be cashed when we have not fulfilled the conditions that would make it payable to us. We present to God His promises, and ask Him to fulfill them, when by so doing He would dishonor His own name.

"The promise is 'If ye abide in Me, and My words abide in you, ye shall ask what ye will, and it shall be done unto you.' John 15:7. And John declares: 'Hereby we do know that we know Him, if we keep His commandments. He that saith, I know Him, and keepeth not His commandments, is a liar, and the truth is not in him. But whoso keepeth His word, in him verily is the love of God perfected.' 1 John 2:3–5.

"One of Christ's last commands to His disciples was 'Love one another as I have loved you.' John 13:34. Do we obey this command, or are we indulging sharp, unchristlike traits of character? If we have in any way grieved or wounded others, it is our duty to confess our fault and seek for reconciliation. This is an essential preparation that we may come before God in faith, to ask His blessing.

"There is another matter too often neglected by those who seek the Lord in prayer. Have you been honest with God? By the prophet Malachi the Lord declares, 'Even from the days of your fathers ye are gone away from Mine ordinances, and have not kept them. Return unto Me, and I will return unto you, saith the Lord of hosts. But ye said, Wherein shall we return? Will a man rob God? Yet ye have robbed Me. But ye say, Wherein have we robbed Thee? In tithes and offerings.' Mal. 3:7, 8.

"As the Giver of every blessing, God claims a certain portion of all we possess. This is His provision to sustain the preaching of the gospel. And by making this return to God, we are to show our appreciation of His gifts. But if we withhold from Him that which is His own, how can we claim His blessing? If we are unfaithful stewards of earthly things, how can we expect Him to entrust us with the things of heaven? It may be that here is the secret of unanswered prayer.

"But the Lord in His great mercy is ready to forgive, and He says, 'Bring ye all the tithes into the storehouse, that there may be meat in Mine house, and prove Me now herewith, . . . if I will not open you the windows of heaven, and pour you out a blessing, that there shall not be room enough to receive it. And I will rebuke the devourer for your sakes, and he shall not destroy the fruits of your ground; neither shall your vine cast her fruit before the time in the field . . . And all nations shall call you blessed; for ye shall be a delightsome land, saith the Lord of hosts.' Mal. 3:10–12.

"So it is with every other one of God's requirements. All His gifts are promised on condition of obedience. God has a heaven full of blessings for those who will co-operate with Him. All who obey Him may with confidence claim the fulfillment of His promises.

"But we must show a firm, undeviating trust in God. Often He delays to answer us in order to try our faith or test the genuineness of our desire. Having asked according to His word, we should believe His promise and press our petitions with a determination that will not be denied.

"God does not say, Ask once, and you shall receive. He bids us ask. Unwearyingly persist in prayer. The persistent asking brings the petitioner into a more earnest attitude, and gives him an increased desire to receive the things for which he asks. Christ said to Martha at the grave of Lazarus, 'If thou wouldest believe, thou shouldest see the glory of God.' John 11:40.

"But many have not a living faith. This is why they do not see more of the power of God. Their weakness is the result of their unbelief. They have more faith in their own working than in the working of God for them. They take themselves into their own keeping. They plan and devise, but pray little, and have little real trust in God. They think they have faith, but it is only the impulse of the moment. Failing to realize their own need, or God's willingness to give, they do not persevere in keeping their requests before the Lord.

"Our prayers are to be as earnest and persistent as was the petition of the needy friend who asked for the loaves at midnight. The more earnestly and steadfastly we ask, the closer will be our spiritual union with Christ. We shall receive increased blessings because we have increased faith.

"Our part is to pray and believe. Watch unto prayer. Watch, and co-operate with the prayer-hearing God. Bear in mind that 'we are labourers together with God.' I Cor. 3:9. Speak and act in harmony with your prayers. It will make an infinite difference with you whether trial shall prove your faith to be genuine, or show that your prayers are only a form.

"When perplexities arise, and difficulties confront you, look not for help to humanity. Trust all with God. The practice of telling our difficulties to others only makes us weak, and brings no strength to them. It lays upon them the burden of our spiritual infirmities, which they cannot relieve. We seek the strength of erring, finite man, when we might have the strength of the unerring, infinite God.

"You need not go to the ends of the earth for wisdom, for God is near. It is not the capabilities you now possess or ever will have that will give you success. It is that which the Lord can do for you. We need to have far less confidence in what man can do and far more confidence in what God can do for every believing soul. He longs to have you reach after Him by faith. He longs to have you expect great things from Him. He longs to give you understanding in temporal as well as in spiritual matters. He can sharpen the intellect. He can give tact and skill. Put your talents into the work, ask God for wisdom, and it will be given you.

"Take the word of Christ as your assurance. Has He not invited you to come unto Him? Never allow yourself to talk in a hopeless, discouraged way. If you do you will lose much. By looking at appearances and complaining when difficulties and pressure come, you give evidence of a sickly, enfeebled faith. Talk and act as if your faith was invincible. The Lord is rich in resources; He owns the world. Look heavenward in faith. Look to Him who has light and power and efficiency.

"There is in genuine faith a buoyancy, a steadfastness of principle, and a fixedness of purpose that neither time nor toil can weaken. 'Even the youths shall faint and be weary, and the young men shall utterly fall: but they that wait upon the Lord shall renew their strength; they shall mount up with wings as eagles; they shall run, and not be weary; and they shall walk, and not faint.' Isa. 40:30, 31.

"There are many who long to help others, but they feel that they have no spiritual strength or light to impart. Let them present their petitions at the throne of grace. Plead for the Holy Spirit. God stands back of every promise He has made. With your Bible in your hands say, I have done as Thou hast said. I present Thy promise, 'Ask, and it shall be given you; seek, and ye shall find; knock, and it shall be opened unto you.'

"We must not only pray in Christ's name, but by the inspiration of the Holy Spirit. This explains what is meant when it is said that the Spirit 'maketh intercession for us, with groanings which cannot be uttered.' Rom. 8:26. Such prayer God delights to answer. When with earnestness and intensity we breathe a prayer in the name of Christ, there is in that very intensity a pledge from God that He is about to answer our prayer 'exceeding abundantly above all that we ask or think.' Eph. 3:20.

"Christ has said, 'What things soever ye desire, when ye pray, believe that ye receive them, and ye shall have them.' Mark 11:24. 'Whatsoever ye shall ask in My name, that will I do, that the Father may be glorified in the Son.' John 14:13. And the beloved John, under the inspiration of the Holy Spirit, speaks with great plainness and assurance: 'If we ask anything according to His will, He heareth us: and if we know that He hear us, whatsoever we ask, we know that we have the petitions that we desired of Him.' I John 5:14, 15. Then press your petition to the Father in the name of Jesus. God will honor that name.

"The rainbow round about the throne is an assurance that God is true, that in Him is no variableness, neither shadow of turning. We have sinned against Him, and are undeserving of His favor; yet He Himself has put into our lips that most wonderful of pleas, 'Do not abhor us, for Thy name's sake; do not disgrace the throne of Thy glory; remember, break not Thy covenant with us.' Jer. 14:21. When we come to Him confessing our unworthiness and sin, He has pledged Himself to give heed to our cry. The honor of His throne is staked for the fulfillment of His word unto us.

"Like Aaron, who symbolized Christ, our Saviour bears the names of all His people on His heart in the holy place. Our great High Priest remembers all the words by which He has encouraged us to trust. He is ever mindful of His covenant.

"All will who seek of Him shall find. All who knock will have the door opened to them. The excuse will not be made, Trouble Me not; the door is closed; I do not wish to open it. Never will one be told, I cannot help you. Those who beg at midnight for loaves to feed the hungry souls will be successful.

"In the parable, he who asks bread for the stranger, receives 'as many as he needeth.' And in what measure will God impart to us that we may impart to others? 'According to the measure of the gift of Christ.' Eph. 4:7. Angels are watching with intense interest to see how man is dealing with his fellow men. When they see one manifest Christlike sympathy for the erring, they press to his side and bring to his remembrance words to speak that will be as the bread of life to the soul. So 'God shall supply all your need according to His riches in glory by Christ Jesus.' Phil. 4:19. Your testimony in its genuineness and reality He will make powerful in the power of the life to come. The word of the Lord will be in your mouth as truth and righteousness.

"Personal effort for others should be preceded by much secret prayer; for it requires great wisdom to understand the science of saving souls. Before communicating with men, commune with Christ. At the throne of heavenly grace obtain a preparation for ministering to the people.

"Let your heart break for the longing it has for God, for the living God. The life of Christ has shown what humanity can do by being partaker of the divine nature. All that Christ received from God we too may

have. Then ask and receive. With the persevering faith of Jacob, with the unyielding
persistence of Elijah, claim for yourself all
that God has promised.

"Let the glorious conceptions of God
possess your mind. Let your life be knit
by hidden links to the life of Jesus. He
who commanded the light to shine out of
darkness is willing to shine in your heart,
to give the light of the knowledge of the
glory of God in the face of Jesus Christ.
The Holy Spirit will take the things of God
and show them unto you, conveying them
as a living power into the obedient heart.
Christ will lead you to the threshold of the
Infinite. You may behold the glory beyond
the veil, and reveal to men the sufficiency
of Him who ever liveth to make intercession for us."—*Christ's Object Lessons,* pp.
142:1–149:3.

**Another look at the conditions—**
"Our heavenly Father waits to bestow
upon us the fullness of His blessing. It is
our privilege to drink largely at the foun-
tain of boundless love. What a wonder it
is that we pray so little! God is ready and
willing to hear the sincere prayer of the
humblest of His children, and yet there is

much manifest reluctance on our part to make known our wants to God. What can the angels of heaven think of poor helpless human beings, who are subject to temptation, when God's heart of infinite love yearns toward them, ready to give them more than they can ask or think, and yet they pray so little and have so little faith? The angels love to bow before God; they love to be near Him. They regard communion with God as their highest joy; and yet the children of earth, who need so much the help that God only can give, seem satisfied to walk without the light of His Spirit, the companionship of His presence.

"The darkness of the evil one incloses those who neglect to pray. The whispered temptations of the enemy entice them to sin; and it is all because they do not make use of the privileges that God has given them in the divine appointment of prayer. Why should the sons and daughters of God be reluctant to pray, when prayer is the key in the hand of faith to unlock heaven's storehouse, where are treasured the boundless resources of Omnipotence? Without unceasing prayer and diligent watching we are in danger of growing careless and of deviating from the right path. The adversary seeks continually to obstruct the way to the mercy seat, that we may not by earnest supplication and faith obtain grace and power to resist temptation.

"There are certain conditions upon which we may expect that God will hear and answer our prayers. One of the first of these is that we feel our need of help from Him. He has promised, 'I will pour water upon him that is thirsty, and floods upon the dry ground.' Isa. 44:3. Those who hunger and thirst after righteousness, who long after God, may be sure that they will be filled. The heart must be open to the Spirit's influence, or God's blessing cannot be received.

"Our great need is itself an argument and pleads most eloquently in our behalf. But the Lord is to be sought unto to do these things for us. He says, 'Ask, and it shall be given you.' And 'He that spared not His own Son, but delivered Him up for us all, how shall He not with Him also freely give us all things?' Matt. 7:7; Rom. 8:32.

"If we regard iniquity in our hearts, if we cling to any known sin, the Lord will not hear us; but the prayer of the penitent, contrite soul is always accepted. When all known wrongs are righted, we may believe that God will answer our petitions. Our own merit will never commend us to the favor of God; it is the worthiness of Jesus that will save us, His blood that will cleanse us; yet we have a work to do in complying with the conditions of acceptance.

"Another element of prevailing prayer is faith. 'He that cometh to God must believe that He is, and that He is a rewarder of them that diligently seek Him.' Heb. 11:6. Jesus said to His disciples, 'What things soever ye desire, when ye pray, believe that ye receive them, and ye shall have them.' Mark 11:24. Do we take Him at His word?

"The assurance is broad and unlimited, and He is faithful who has promised. When we do not receive the very things we asked for, at the time we ask, we are still to believe that the Lord hears and that He will answer our prayers. We are so erring and short-sighted that we some-times ask for things that would not be a blessing to us, and our heavenly Father in love answers our prayers by giving us that which will be for our highest good—that which we ourselves would desire if with vision divinely enlightened we could see all things as they really are. When our prayers seem not to be answered, we are to cling to the promise; for the time of answering will surely come, and we shall receive the blessing we need most. But to claim that prayer will always be answered in the very way and for the particular thing that we desire, is presumption. God is too wise to err, and too good to withhold any good thing from them that walk uprightly. Then do not fear to trust Him, even though you do not see the immediate answer to your prayers. Rely upon His sure promise, 'Ask, and it shall be given you.'

"If we take counsel with our doubts and fears, or try to solve everything that we cannot see clearly, before we have faith, perplexities will only increase and deepen. But if we come to God, feeling helpless and dependent, as we really are, and in humble, trusting faith make known our wants to Him whose knowledge is infinite, who sees everything in creation, and who governs everything by His will and word, He can and will attend to our cry, and will let light shine into our hearts. Through sincere prayer we are brought into connection with the mind of the Infinite. We may have no remarkable evidence at the time that the face of our Redeemer is bending over us in compassion and love; but this is even so. We may not feel His visible touch, but His hand is upon us in love and pitying tenderness.

"When we come to ask mercy and blessing from God we should have a spirit of love and forgiveness in our hearts. How can we pray, 'Forgive us our debts, as we forgive our debtors,' (Matt 6:12) and yet indulge an unforgiving spirit? If we expect our own prayers to be heard we must forgive others in the same manner and to the same extent as we hope to be forgiven.

"Perseverance in prayer has been made a condition of receiving. We must pray always if we would grow in faith and experience. We are to be 'instant in prayer,' to 'continue in prayer, and watch in the same with thanksgiving.' Rom. 12:12; Col. 4:2. Peter exhorts believers to be 'sober, and watch unto prayer.' 1 Peter 4:7. Paul directs, 'In everything by prayer and supplication with thanksgiving let your requests be made known unto God.' Phil. 4:6. 'But ye, beloved,' says Jude, 'praying in the Holy Ghost, keep yourselves in the love of God.' Jude 20, 21. Unceasing prayer is the unbroken union of the soul with God, so that life from God flows into our life; and from our life, purity and holiness flow back to God.

"There is necessity for diligence in prayer; let nothing hinder you. Make every effort to keep open the communion between Jesus and your own soul. Seek every opportunity to go where prayer is wont to be made. Those who are really seeking for communion with God will be seen in the prayer meeting, faithful to do their duty and earnest and anxious to reap all the benefits they can gain. They will improve every opportunity of placing themselves where they can receive the rays of light from heaven.

"We should pray in the family circle, and above all we must not neglect secret prayer, for this is the life of the soul. It is impossible for the soul to flourish while prayer is neglected. Family or public prayer alone is not sufficient. In solitude let the soul be laid open to the inspecting eye of God. Secret prayer is to be heard only by the prayer-hearing God. No curious ear is to receive the burden of such petitions. In secret prayer the soul is free from surrounding influences, free from excitement. Calmly, yet fervently, will it reach out after God. Sweet and abiding will be the influence emanating from Him who seeth in secret, whose ear is open to hear the prayer arising from the heart. By calm, simple faith the soul holds communion with God and gathers to itself rays of divine light to strengthen and sustain it in the conflict with Satan. God is our tower of strength.

"Pray in your closet, and as you go about your daily labor let your heart be often uplifted to God. It was thus that Enoch walked with God. These silent prayers rise like precious incense before the throne of grace. Satan cannot overcome him whose heart is thus stayed upon God."—*Steps to Christ,* pp. 94:1–99:0.

**At certain times, fasting also**—"For certain things, fasting and prayer are recommended and appropriate. In the hand of God they are a means of cleansing the heart and promoting a receptive frame of mind. We obtain answers to our prayers because we humble our souls before God.

"It is in the order of God that those who bear responsibilities should often meet together to counsel with one another and to pray earnestly for that wisdom which He alone can impart. Unitedly make known your troubles to God. Talk less; much precious time is lost in talk that brings no light. Let brethren unite in fasting and prayer for the wisdom that God has promised to supply liberally.

"Whenever it is necessary for the advancement of the cause of truth and the glory of God, that an opponent be met, how carefully, and with what humility, should they [the advocates of truth] go into the conflict. With heart searching, confession of sin, and earnest prayer, and often fasting for a time, they should entreat that God would especially help them, and give His saving, precious truth a glorious victory, that error might appear in its true deformity, and its advocates be completely discomfited.

"The true fasting which should be recommended to all, is abstinence from every stimulating kind of food, and the proper use of wholesome, simple food, which God has provided in abundance. Men need to think less about what they shall eat and drink of temporal food, and much more in regard to the food from heaven, that will give tone and vitality to the whole religious experience.

"Now and onward till the close of time the people of God should be more earnest, more wide-awake, not trusting in their own wisdom, but in the wisdom of their Leader. They should set aside days for fasting and prayer. Entire abstinence from food may not be required, but they should eat sparingly of the most simple food.

"All the fasting in the world will not take the place of simple trust in the word of God. 'Ask,' He says, 'and ye shall receive' . . You are not called upon to fast 40 days. The Lord bore that fast for you in the wilderness of temptation. There would be no virtue in such a fast; but there is virtue in the blood of Christ.

"The spirit of true fasting and prayer is the spirit which yields mind, heart, and will to God."—*Counsels on Diet and Foods,* pp. 187:6–189:2.

**Examine your own heart**—"Closely examine your own heart, and the state of your affections toward God. Inquire, Have I devoted the precious moments of today in seeking to please myself, seeking for my own amusement? or have I made others happy? Have I helped those connected with me to greater devotion to God and to appreciate eternal things? Have I brought my religion into my home, and there revealed the grace of Christ in my words and in my deportment? By my respectful obedience, have I honored my parents, and thus kept the fifth commandment? Have I cheerfully taken up my little, everyday duties, performing them with fidelity, doing what I could to lighten the burdens of others? Have I kept my lips from evil, and my tongue from speaking guile? Have I honored Christ my Redeemer, who gave

His precious life that eternal life might be within my reach?

"At the beginning of the day, do not, dear youth, neglect to pray earnestly to Jesus that He will impart to you strength and grace to resist the temptations of the enemy in whatever form they may come; and if you pray earnestly, in faith and contrition of soul, the Lord will hear your prayer. But you must watch as well as pray. Jesus has said: 'Ask, and it shall be given you; seek, and ye shall find; knock, and it shall be opened unto you: for every one that asketh receiveth; and he that seeketh findeth; and to him that knocketh it shall be opened. Or what man is there of you, whom, if his son ask bread, will he give him a stone? Or if he ask a fish, will he give him a serpent? If ye then, being evil, know how to give good gifts unto your children, how much more shall your Father which is in heaven give good things to them that ask Him?'

"Children and youth may come to Jesus with their burdens and perplexities, and know that He will respect their appeals to Him, and give them the very things they need. Be earnest; be resolute. Present the promise of God, and then believe without a doubt. Do not wait to feel special emotions before you think the Lord answers. Do not mark out some particular way that the Lord must work for you before you believe you receive the things you ask of Him; but trust His word, and leave the whole matter in the hands of the Lord, with full faith that your prayer will be honored, and the answer will come at the very time and in the very way your heavenly Father sees is for your good; and then live out your prayers. Walk humbly and keep moving forward.

" 'For the Lord God is a sun and shield: the Lord will give grace and glory: no good thing will He withhold from them that walk uprightly.' Ps. 84:11.

" 'O fear the Lord, ye His saints: for there is no want to them that fear Him. The young lions do lack, and suffer hunger: but they that seek the Lord shall not want any good thing.' Ps. 34:9, 10.

" 'Keep thy tongue from evil, and thy lips from speaking guile. Depart from evil, and do good; seek peace, and pursue it. The eyes of the Lord are upon the righteous, and His ears are open unto their cry. The face of the Lord is against them that do evil, to cut off the remembrance of them from the earth. The righteous cry, and the Lord heareth, and delivereth them out of all their troubles. The Lord is nigh unto them that are of a broken heart; and saveth such as be of a contrite spirit.' Ps. 34:13–18.

"Here are promises, rich and abundant, upon conditions that you cease to do evil and learn to do well. Then set your aim in life high, as did Joseph and Daniel and Moses; and take into consideration the cost of character-building, and then build for time and for eternity . .

"We are weak and without wisdom, but God has said: 'If any of you lack wisdom, let him ask of God, that giveth to all men liberally, and upbraideth not; and it shall be given him.' James 1:5. Only learn to be thorough, never to let go your hold upon God, to persevere in His service, and you will be an overcomer through the blood of the Lamb."—*Messages to Young People,* pp. 122:1–124:4.

**Pray for the Holy Spirit to use you**—"A revival of true godliness among us is the greatest and most urgent of all our needs. To seek this should be our first work. There must be earnest effort to obtain the blessing of the Lord, not because God is not willing to bestow His blessing upon us, but because we are unprepared to receive it. Our heavenly Father is more willing to give His Holy Spirit to them that ask Him, than are earthly parents to give good gifts to their children. But it is our work, by confession, humiliation, repentance, and earnest prayer, to fulfill the conditions upon which God has promised to grant us His blessing. A revival need be expected only in answer to prayer. While the people are so destitute of God's Holy Spirit, they cannot appreciate the preaching of the Word; but when the Spirit's power touches their hearts, then the discourses given will not be without effect. Guided by the teachings of God's Word, with the manifestations of His Spirit, in the exercise of sound discretion, those who attend our meetings will gain a precious experience, and returning home, will be prepared to exert a healthful influence.

"The old standard bearers knew what it was to wrestle with God in prayer, and to enjoy the outpouring of His Spirit. But these are passing off from the stage of action; and who are coming up to fill their places? How is it with the rising generation? Are they converted to God? Are we awake to the work that is going on in the heavenly sanctuary, or are we waiting for some compelling power to come upon the church before we shall arouse? Are we hoping to see the whole church revived? That time will never come.

"There are persons in the church who are not converted, and who will not unite in earnest, prevailing prayer. We must enter upon the work individually. We must pray more, and talk less. Iniquity abounds, and the people must be taught not to be satisfied with a form of godliness without the spirit and power. If we are intent upon searching our own hearts, putting away our sins, and correcting our evil tendencies, our souls will not be lifted up unto vanity; we shall be distrustful of ourselves, having an abiding sense that our sufficiency is of God.

"We have far more to fear from within than from without. The hindrances to strength and success are far greater from the church itself than from the world. Unbelievers have a right to expect that those who profess to be keeping the commandments of God and the faith of Jesus, will do more than any other class to promote and honor, by their consistent lives, by their godly example and their active influence, the cause which they represent. But how often have the professed advocates of the truth proved the greatest obstacle to its advancement! The unbelief indulged, the doubts expressed, the darkness cherished, encourage the presence of evil angels, and open the way for the accomplishment of Satan's devices." —*1 Selected Messages,* pp. 121:1–122:3.

**That which brings divine power—** "The end of all things is at hand. What we have done must not be allowed to place the period to our work. The Captain of our salvation says, 'Advance. The night cometh, in which no man can work.' Constantly we are to increase in usefulness. Our lives are always to be under the power of Christ . .

"Prayer is a heaven-ordained means of success. Appeals, petitions, entreaties, between man and man, move men, and act as a part in controlling the affairs of nations. But prayer moves heaven. That power alone that comes in answer to prayer will make men wise in the wisdom of heaven, and enable them to work in the unity of the Spirit, joined together by the bonds of peace. Prayer, faith, confidence in God, bring a divine power that sets human calculations at their real worth,—nothingness."—*Sons and Daughters of God*, p. 335:2–3.

**Begin the morning with prayer—** "The very first outbreathing of the soul in the morning should be for the presence of Jesus. 'Without Me,' He says, 'ye can do nothing.' It is Jesus that we need; His light, His life, His spirit, must be ours continually. We need Him every hour. And we should pray in the morning that as the sun illuminates the landscape, and fills the world with light, so the Sun of Righteousness may shine into the chambers of mind and heart, and make us all light in the Lord. We cannot do without His presence one moment. The enemy knows when we undertake to do without our Lord, and he is there, ready to fill our minds with his evil suggestions that we may fall from our steadfastness; but it is the desire of the Lord that from moment to moment we should abide in Him, and thus be complete in Him."—*Bible Echo,* January 15, 1892.

**Cultivate the habit**—"Cultivate the habit of talking with the Saviour . . . . Let the heart be continually uplifted in silent petition for help, for light, for strength, for knowledge. Let every breath be a prayer."—*Ministry of Healing,* pp. 510:1–511:0.

**Pray everywhere**—"Those who teach and preach the most effectively are those who wait humbly upon God, and watch hungrily for His guidance and His grace. Watch, pray, work—this is the Christian's watchword. The life of a true Christian is a life of constant prayer. He knows that the light and strength of one day is not sufficient for the trials and conflicts of the next. Satan is continually changing his temptations. Every day we shall be placed in different circumstances; and in the untried scenes that await us we shall be surrounded by fresh dangers, and constantly assailed by new and unexpected temptations. It is only through the strength and grace gained from heaven that we can hope to meet the temptations and perform the duties before us.

"It is a wonderful thing that we can pray effectually; that unworthy, erring mortals possess the power of offering their requests to God. What higher power can man desire than this,—to be linked with the infinite God? Feeble, sinful man has the privilege of speaking to his Maker. We may utter words that reach the throne of the Monarch of the universe. We may speak with Jesus as we walk by the way, and He says, I am at thy right hand [see Ps. 16:8].

"We may commune with God in our hearts; we may walk in companionship with Christ. When engaged in our daily labor, we may breathe out our heart's desire, inaudible to any human ear; but that word cannot die away into silence, nor can it be lost. Nothing can drown the soul's desire. It rises above the din of the street, above the noise of machinery. It is God to whom we are speaking, and our prayer is heard.

"Ask, then; ask, and ye shall receive. Ask for humility, wisdom, courage, increase of faith. To every sincere prayer an answer will come. It may not come just as you desire, or at the time you look for it; but it will come in the way and at the time that will best meet your need. The prayers you offer in loneliness, in weariness, in trial, God answers, not always according to your expectations, but always for your good."—*Gospel Workers,* 1915, pp. 257:3–258:3.

**The greatest victories**—"The greatest victories to the church of Christ or to the individual Christian . . are those victories that are gained in the audience chamber with God, when earnest, agonizing faith lays hold upon the mighty arm of power."— *Patriarchs and Prophets,* p. 203:1.

**Victories for the youth**—"The young would not be seduced into sin if they would refuse to enter any path save that upon which they could ask God's blessing."— *Great Controversy,* p. 622:3.

**More victories for the youth**—"By constant prayer, the youth may obtain principles so firm that the most powerful temptations will not draw them from their allegiance to God."—*Youth's Instructor,* February 15, 1900, para 1.

**You are invited to come**—"You are invited to come, to ask, to seek, to knock; and you are assured that you will not come in vain. Jesus says, 'Ask, and it shall be given you; seek, and ye shall find; knock, and it shall be opened unto you: for everyone that asketh receiveth; and he that seeketh findeth; and to him that knocketh it shall be opened.' Matt. 7:7, 8.

"Christ illustrates the willingness of God to bless by the willingness of a father to grant the request of his child . . . [Luke 11:11–13, quoted].

"We come to God in the name of Jesus by special invitation, and He welcomes us to His audience chamber. He imparts to the humble, contrite soul that faith in Christ by which he is justified. Jesus blots out as a thick cloud his transgressions, and the comforted heart exclaims, 'O Lord, I will praise Thee: though Thou wast angry with me, Thine anger is turned away, and Thou comfortedst me.' Isaiah 12:1. Such a one will understand by his own experience the words of Paul, 'With the heart man believeth unto righteousness; and with the mouth confession is made unto salvation.' Romans 10:10.

"Man then becomes an agent whom God can employ to work out His purposes. He represents Christ, holding forth to the world His mercy and love. He has a testimony that he desires others to hear. In the language of the psalmist he says, 'Bless the Lord, O my soul: and all that is within me, bless His holy name. Bless the Lord, O my soul, and forget not all His benefits: who forgiveth all thine iniquities; who healeth all thy diseases; who redeemeth thy life from destruction; who crowneth thee with loving-kindness and tender mercies.' Psalm 103:1–4."—*Counsels to Parents, Teachers, and Students,* pp. 242:1–4—243:0.

**At certain times a holy Presence—** "There have been times when the blessing of God has been bestowed in answer to prayer, so that when others have come into the room, no sooner did they step over the threshold than they exclaimed, 'The Lord is here!' Not a word had been uttered, but the blessed influence of God's holy presence was sensibly felt. The joy that comes from Jesus Christ was there; and in this sense the Lord had been in the room just as verily as He walked through the streets of Jerusalem, or appeared to the disciples when they were in the upper chamber, and said, 'Peace be unto you.' " —*My Life Today,* p. 51:5.

**Earnest, believing prayer**—"We have too little faith. We limit the Holy One of Israel. We should be grateful that God condescends to use any of us as His instruments. For every earnest prayer put up in faith for anything, answers will be returned. They may not come just as we have expected; but they will come—not perhaps as we have devised, but at the very time when we most need them. But, oh, how sinful is our unbelief! 'If ye abide in Me, and My words abide in you, ye shall ask what ye will, and it shall be done unto you.' John 15:7."—*Life Sketches of Ellen White,* p. 207:2.

**That which no other power can accomplish**— "Prayer and faith will do what no power on earth can accomplish. We are seldom, in all respects, placed in the same position twice."—*Ministry of Healing,* p. 509:2.

**Part of God's plan**—"It is a part of God's plan to grant us, in answer to the prayer of faith, that which He would not bestow did we not thus ask."—*Great Controversy*, p. 525:2.

**We must climb the prayer ladder ourselves**—"After we have offered our petitions, we are to answer them ourselves as far as possible, and not wait for God to do for us what we can do for ourselves. The help is to be combined with human effort, aspiration, and energy. But we cannot reach the battlements of heaven without climbing for ourselves. We cannot be borne up by the prayers of others when we ourselves neglect to pray; for God has made no such provision for us . . . . The unlovely traits in our characters are not removed, and replaced by traits that are pure and lovely, without some effort on our part."—*Bible Echo*, November 1887.

**Ask for that which you cannot do for yourself**—"Ask God to do for you those things that you cannot do for yourselves. Tell Jesus everything. Lay open before Him the secrets of your heart; for His eye searches the inmost recesses of the soul, and He reads your thoughts as an open book. When you have asked for the things that are necessary for your soul's good, believe that you receive them, and you shall have them. Accept His gifts with your whole heart; for Jesus has died that you might have the precious things of heaven as your own, and at last find a home with the heavenly angels in the kingdom of God."—*Youth's Instructor,* July 7, 1892, para 4.

**This is the prayer of faith**—"The prayer that comes from an earnest heart, when the simple wants of the soul are expressed just as we would ask an earthly friend for a favor, expecting that it would be granted—this is the prayer of faith."—*Bible Echo,* November 1887.

**The prayers of mothers**—"Those who keep the law of God look upon their children with indefinable feelings of hope and fear, wondering what part they will act in the great conflict that is just before them. The anxious mother questions, 'What stand will they take? What can I do to prepare them to act well their part, so that they will be the recipients of eternal glory?'

"Great responsibilities rest upon you, mothers . . . . You may aid them to develop characters that will not be swayed or influenced to do evil, but will sway and influence others to do right. By your fervent prayers of faith you can move the arm that moves the world . . . .

"The prayers of Christian mothers are not disregarded by the Father of all . . He will not turn away your petitions, and leave you and yours to the buffetings of Satan in the great day of final conflict. It is for you to work with simplicity and faithfulness, and God will establish the work of your hands.

"The lifework performed on earth is acknowledged in the heavenly courts as a work well done. With joy unutterable, parents see the crown, the robe, the harp, given to their children . . . . The seed sown with tears and prayers may have seemed to be sown in vain, but their harvest is reaped with joy at last. Their children have been redeemed.

"When the 'well done' of the great Judge is pronounced, and the crown of immortal glory is placed upon the brow of the victor, many will raise their crowns in sight of the assembled universe and, pointing to their mothers, say, 'She made me all I am through the grace of God. Her instruction, her prayers, have been blessed

to my eternal salvation.' "—*My Life Today,*
p. 21:1–5.

**How they prayed during the Midnight Cry**—"At that time there was faith that brought answers to prayer—faith that had respect to the recompense of reward. Like showers of rain upon the thirsty earth, the Spirit of grace descended upon the earnest seekers. Those who expected soon to stand face to face with their Redeemer felt a solemn joy that was unutterable. The softening, subduing power of the Holy Spirit melted the heart as His blessing was bestowed in rich measure upon the faithful, believing ones.

"Carefully and solemnly those who received the message came up to the time when they hoped to meet their Lord. Every morning they felt that it was their first duty to secure the evidence of their acceptance with God. Their hearts were closely united, and they prayed much with and for one another. They often met together in secluded places to commune with God, and the voice of intercession ascended to heaven from the fields and groves. The assurance of the Saviour's approval was more necessary to them than their daily food; and if a cloud darkened their minds, they did not rest until it was swept away. As they felt the witness of pardoning grace, they longed to behold Him whom their souls loved."—*The Great Controversy,* pp. 402:3–403:1.

**More on the Midnight Cry experience**—"Heaven is not closed against the fervent prayers of the righteous. Elijah was a man subject to like passions as we are, yet the Lord heard, and in a most striking manner answered his petitions. The only reason for our lack of power with God is to be found in ourselves. If the inner life of many who profess the truth were presented before them, they would not claim to be Christians. They are not growing in grace. A hurried prayer is offered now and then, but their is no real communion with God.

"We must be much in prayer if we would make progress in the divine life. When the message of truth was first proclaimed, how much we prayed. How often was the voice of intercession heard in the chamber, in the barn, in the orchard, or the grove. Frequently we spent hours in earnest prayer, two or three together claiming the promise; often the sound of weeping was heard and then the voice of thanksgiving and the song of praise. Now the day of God is nearer than when we first believed, and we should be more earnest, more zealous, and fervent than in those early days. Our perils are greater now than then. Souls are more hardened. We need now to be imbued with the Spirit of Christ, and we should not rest until we receive it."—*5 Testimonies,* pp. 161:3–162:0.

**Those who bear the final message**—"If the messengers who bear the last solemn warning to the world would pray for the blessing of God, not in a cold, listless, lazy manner, but fervently and in faith, as did Jacob, they would find many places where they could say, 'I have seen God face to face, and my life is preserved.' Gen 32:30. They could be accounted of heaven as princes, having power to prevail with God and with men."—*Great Controversy,* p. 622:3.

**Others who obtained answers**—"The patriarchs were men of prayer, and God did great things for them. When Jacob left his father's house for a strange land, he prayed in humble contrition, and in the night season the Lord answered him through vision . . . . The Lord comforted the lonely wanderer with precious promises; and protecting angels were represented as stationed on each side of his path . . . .

"Joseph prayed, and he was preserved from sin amid influences that were calculated to lead him away from God. When tempted to leave the path of purity and uprightness, he rejected the suggestion with, 'How can I do this great wickedness, and sin against God?'

"Moses, who was much in prayer, was known as the meekest man on the face of the earth . . . . While he was leading the children of Israel through the wilderness, again and again it seemed that they must be exterminated on account of their murmuring and rebellion. But Moses went to the true Source of power; he laid the case before the Lord . . . . And the Lord said, 'I have pardoned according to thy word' . . . .

"Daniel was a man of prayer, and God gave him wisdom and firmness to resist every influence that conspired to draw him into the snare of intemperance. Even in his youth he was a moral giant in the strength of the Mighty One . . . .

"In the prison at Philippi, while suffering from the cruel stripes they had received, their feet fast in the stocks, Paul and Silas prayed and sang praise to God, and angels were sent from heaven to deliver them."— *My Life Today,* p. 20:2–6.

We invite you to view the complete
selection of titles we publish at:

www.TEACHServices.com

or write or email us your praises,
reactions, or thoughts about this
or any other book we publish at:

**TEACH Services, Inc.**
P.O. Box 954
Ringgold, GA 30736

info@TEACHServices.com

Finally, if you are interested in seeing
your own book in print, please contact us at

publishing@teachservices.com.

We would be happy to review your manuscript for free.

CPSIA information can be obtained at www.ICGtesting.com
Printed in the USA
LVOW030957011211

257243LV00005B/8/P

9 781572 585232